P9-DFJ-268

DRUMS and PERCUSSION Instruments

by ANITA GANERI

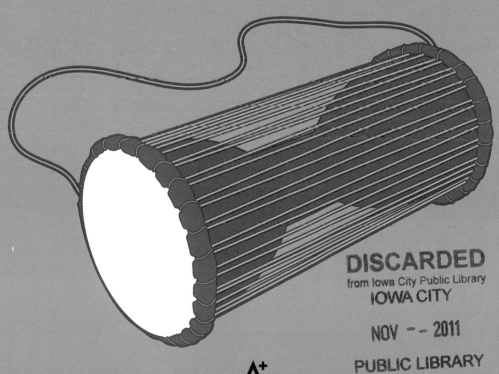

DISCARDED
from Iowa City Public Library
IOWA CITY

NOV -- 2011

PUBLIC LIBRARY

A⁺
Smart Apple Media

Published by Smart Apple Media
P.O. Box 3263, Mankato, Minnesota 56002

U.S. publication copyright © 2012 Smart Apple Media. International copyright reserved in all countries.
No part of this book may be reproduced in any form without written permission from the publisher.

Printed in the United States of America at Corporate Graphics, in North Mankato, Minnesota.

Library of Congress Cataloging-in-Publication Data
Ganeri, Anita, 1961-
 Drums and percussion instruments / by Anita Ganeri.
     p. cm. — (How the world makes music)
 Includes index.
 Summary: "Describes various percussion instruments from around the world,
including current drum kits, orchestral instruments such as the xylophone, and
more traditional drums from Africa and Asia."—Provided by publisher.
   ISBN 978-1-59920-478-9 (library binding)
1. Percussion instruments—Juvenile literature. I. Title.
 ML1030.G35 2010
 786.8'19--dc22

                                            2010043356

Created by Appleseed Editions, Ltd.
Designed by Guy Callaby
Illustrated by Graham Rosewarne
Edited by Jinny Johnson
Picture research by Su Alexander

Picture credits:
l = left, r = right, t = top, b = bottom
Title page (left to right) Joost Bazelmans/Shutterstock, Heiner Heine/Photolibrary Group, Lawrence
Wee/Shutterstock, Anyka/Shutterstock; Contents page GFC Collection/Alamy; Page 4 Odile Noel/
Lebrecht Music & Arts; 5 Cheryl Casey/Shutterstock; 6 Dave Bartruff/Photolibrary Group; 8 Heiner
Heine/Photolibrary Group; 9 Michael Freeman/Corbis; 10 Richard Levine/Alamy; 11 Matt Jones/
Alamy; 12 & 13 Lebrecht Music & Arts Picture Library/Alamy; 15 GFC Collection/Alamy; 16 Joost
Bazelmans/Shutterstock; 17l Peter Gudella/Shutterstock, r Aleksko/Shutterstock; 19t Gina Smith/
Shutterstock, b Mediacolour's/Alamy; 20 Lawrence Wee/Shutterstock; 21 Chen Wei Seng/
Shutterstock; 22 Anyka/Shutterstock; 23 Iofoto/Shutterstock; 24 Yanik Chauvin/Shutterstock; 25
Johan Pienaar/Shutterstock; 26 MoMo Productions/Getty Images; 27 Spitfirefoto/Alamy; 28
Lebrecht Music & Arts Picture Library/Alamy
Front cover: Main photo, Boy with cymbals, MoMo Productions/Getty Images; Grayscale b/g pic of
drummer, Benis Arapovic/Shutterstock; Drummer, Joost Bazelmans/Shutterstock; Gong player,
Gina Smith/Shutterstock; Xylophone player, Yanik Chauvin/Shutterstock; Castanets lady, Anyka/
Shutterstock

DAD0047
3-2011

9 8 7 6 5 4 3 2 1

Contents

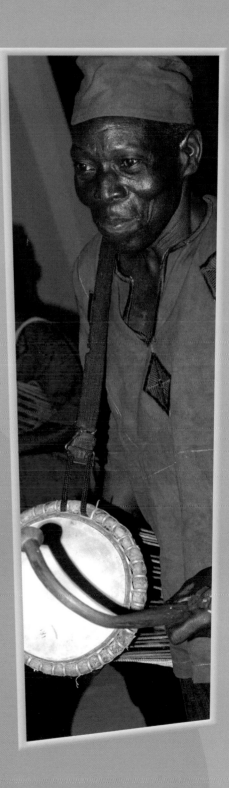

Drums and Percussion

People around the world play musical instruments and sing songs. They use music to show how they feel and as part of festivals and other special occasions. People enjoy music as part of their daily lives.

Rhythm Section

There are many different types of musical instruments. This book is about drums and percussion instruments, from simple wooden blocks to sets of steel drums. These instruments make sounds by being hit, shaken, or scraped. They are used to beat out a rhythm and to add loud, dramatic sound effects to a piece of music. In some parts of the world, drums are also used for sending messages.

This is the percussion section in a school orchestra. Percussion instruments can be made from different materials, including wood, metal, and bone.

Musical Notes

Percussion instruments may have been among the earliest musical instruments ever played. Thousands of years ago, people clapped their hands, stomped their feet, or hit rocks and logs with sticks to make music.

These early percussion instruments are made from wood.

Percussion Instruments in an Orchestra

Timpani

Snare drum

Bass drum

Cymbals

Tam-tam

Triangle

Tambourine

Glockenspiel

Xylophone

Chimes

Tambourine and Triangle

Metal jingles

Drumhead

A tambourine is made from plastic or wood, with a plastic or skin drumhead and metal jingles around the outside. It is shaken or hit with a beater or the hand. A triangle is made from metal and is struck with a metal beater.

Beater

Steel Drum

A steel drum is a type of drum that comes from the island of Trinidad, in the Caribbean. A group of drums and drummers is called a steel band. Steel bands play at parties and in street processions, especially during Carnival time.

Playing a Steel Drum

Drummers use rubber-tipped drumsticks to play their drums and make a rich, metallic sound. They may play two or more drums at the same time. There is no fixed pattern for the notes, so they have to remember the layout of the panels on each drum.

Young musicians are playing steel drums at an outdoor festival on a Caribbean island.

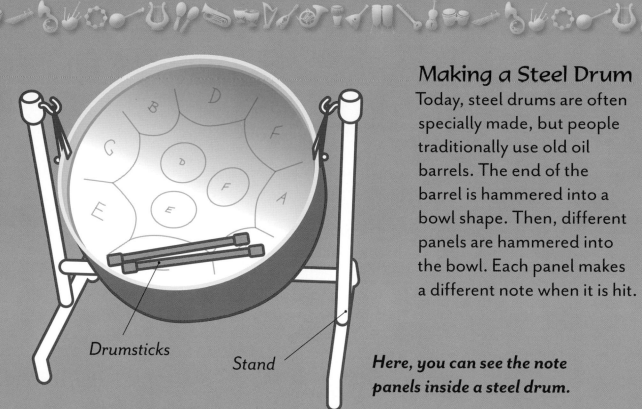

Drumsticks

Stand

Making a Steel Drum

Today, steel drums are often specially made, but people traditionally use old oil barrels. The end of the barrel is hammered into a bowl shape. Then, different panels are hammered into the bowl. Each panel makes a different note when it is hit.

Here, you can see the note panels inside a steel drum.

Musical Notes

There are five main types of steel drums, or pans. They range from the bass drum, which makes the lowest sounds, to the ping-pong, also called the lead or tenor pan, which makes the highest. A bass drum may have only three or four panels, but a lead pan has about 32.

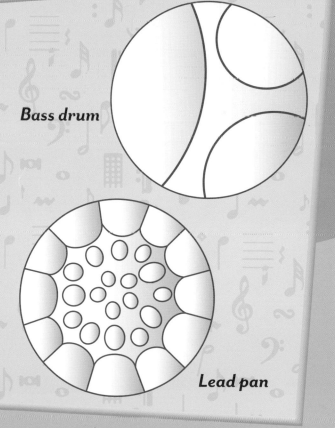

Bass drum

Lead pan

Tabla

The tabla is an instrument used in Indian music to beat out the rhythm. It is made up of two drums, one large and one small. The smaller drum is called the dayan and is made of wood. The larger drum is called the bayan. It is made from wood, metal, or clay. Both drums are covered in goatskin, which is attached to the drum with leather straps.

The dayan (left) has wooden blocks between the straps and drum. These can be adjusted to make different sounds. The bayan (right) makes a deeper sound than the dayan.

Tabla Playing

A tabla player usually sits cross-legged on the floor. He hits the center of the drums with his fingers while pressing down with the palms of his hands. This allows him to change the notes. The drums are placed on ring-shaped cushions so they don't move around.

The tabla is often played as accompaniment to a stringed instrument called the sitar (above left).

Musical Notes

There is a large black spot in the middle of each drum. This is made from a paste of rice, ink, and iron filings and is painted on and left to dry. The spot gives a bell-like sound when it is hit.

Dayan

Black spot

Bayan

Wooden block

Strap

Tuning hammer

Cushion

Bass Drum

Bass drums are the biggest type of drums and make low, deep sounds. They are played in marching bands to mark time. The marchers march to the bass drum's beat. Bass drums are also played in bands and orchestras.

Playing a Bass Drum

The player wears a special harness so that he can carry the drum while he is marching. He straps the drum to his front, with the drumheads facing to the sides. He holds a drumstick in each hand and walks along, beating a rhythm on the drum.

A bass drum is made from a round cylinder with skin stretched over both heads.

Musical Notes

Marching bands were originally groups of musicians who went into battle with armies. They used music for sending signals and for keeping up the soldiers' spirits.

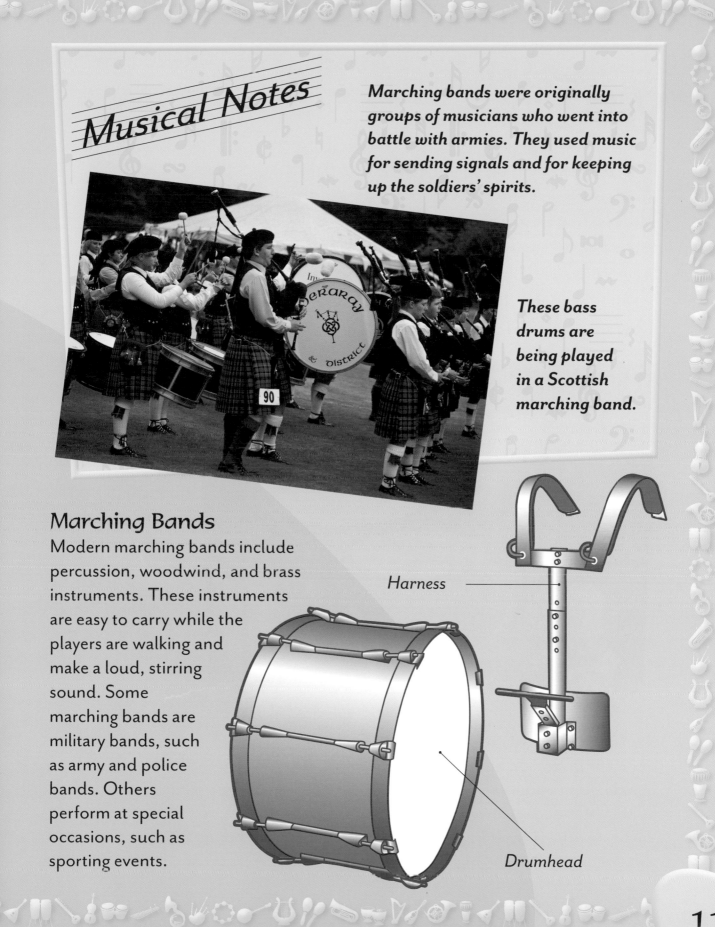

These bass drums are being played in a Scottish marching band.

Marching Bands

Modern marching bands include percussion, woodwind, and brass instruments. These instruments are easy to carry while the players are walking and make a loud, stirring sound. Some marching bands are military bands, such as army and police bands. Others perform at special occasions, such as sporting events.

Harness

Drumhead

Kettledrum

Kettledrums are made from skins stretched over large bowls. The bowls can be metal, fiberglass, wood, clay, or even hollowed-out gourds. There are many different kinds of kettledrums, played all over the world. Some are played with the hands. Others are played with a pair of small cloth-covered mallets.

These are a set of timpani being played in the percussion section of an orchestra.

In the Orchestra

Kettledrums called timpani are played in orchestras and bands. A set of timpani is made of several drums. They are arranged in a semi-circle around the timpanist, from the highest to the lowest drums. The timpanist uses a foot pedal to tune the drums and make different sounds.

Musical Notes

A timpanist can sound a drum roll by striking the drum very quickly, using the left-hand, then right-hand mallets, one after the other.

Skin

Bowl

Foot pedal

Musical Notes

An ancient bronze kettledrum in Bali is said to be the wheel of a chariot that pulled the Moon across the sky. One day, it broke off and fell to Earth.

Talking Drum

Drums can be used to send messages, as well as for making music. "Talking" drums have been used in Africa for hundreds of years for sending messages and greetings from village to village. Their sound can be heard many miles away.

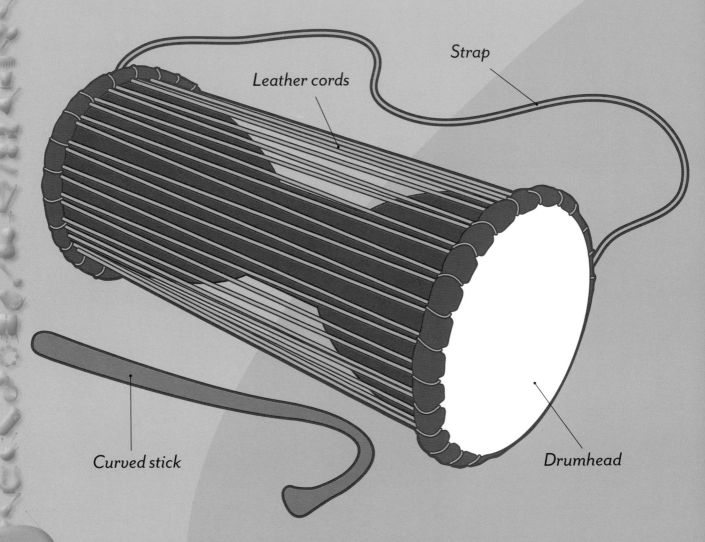

Strap

Leather cords

Curved stick

Drumhead

Kalungu

The kalungu is a famous talking drum from Nigeria. It is shaped like an hourglass, with a head at either end and is made from wood and animal skin. Long leather cords run down the sides of the drum, connecting one end of the drum to the other. The drummer squeezes the cords with his arm to change the drum's pitch. This makes higher or lower notes.

Musical Notes

Talking drums have their own language. They do not make words, but copy the sounds of the languages spoken by the local people.

The drummer holds the drum under his arm, then strikes it with a curved stick.

Drum Set

A drum set is a collection of drums and cymbals played by one person. Drum sets, also called drum kits or trap sets, are played in many rock and pop bands.

Being a drummer in a rock band takes a lot of energy and coordination.

Parts of a Drum Set

1. *Crash cymbal.* A cymbal on a stand that makes a loud, sharp, crashing sound when it is hit with a drumstick.

2. *Tom-toms.* Small drums mounted above the bass drum. They make a high, mellow sound.

3. *Hi hat.* A pair of cymbals on a stand. The drummer presses a pedal to make the cymbals crash together.

6. *Floor tom.* A large tom-tom that usually stands on the floor on three legs. It gives a low, deep sound.

4. *Snare drum.* A drum with wires stretched across the bottom. When the drum is hit, the wires vibrate and make a cracking sound.

5. *Bass drum.* A large drum that stands on its side. It is played with a mallet worked by pressing on a pedal.

Musical Notes

Drumsticks

Brushes

Drummers mainly use drumsticks or brushes for playing. Drumsticks make a louder sound. Brushes give a quieter sound.

Gong

Gongs are popular percussion instruments, particularly in Southeast Asia. They are used in musical performances and in religious ceremonies. They were first played in China about 1,500 years ago. Gongs, called tam-tams, are also played in western orchestras.

Musical Notes

It is thought that gongs were first used in China to call farm workers in from the fields.

Playing a Gong

A gong is a large disc of metal that hangs from its rim on a stand. In the middle of the gong, there is a raised part, called the boss. The player hits the boss with a wooden stick that has a soft, felt-covered head. If the gong is hit hard, it booms loudly as it vibrates. If it is struck more softly, it makes a gentle sound.

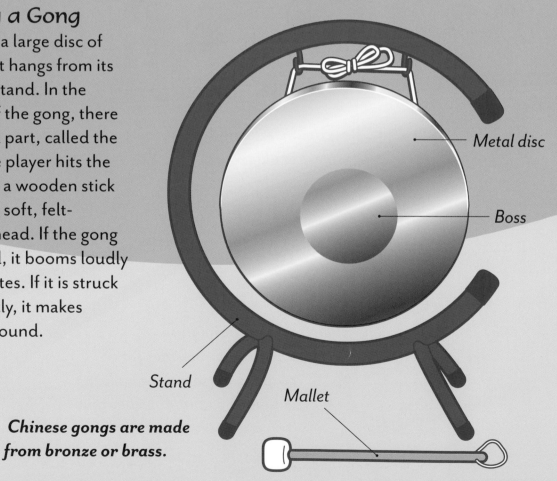

Metal disc

Boss

Stand

Mallet

Chinese gongs are made from bronze or brass.

18

A man strikes a gong at a shrine during a festival in Thailand.

Musical Notes

In a Chinese opera, a gong is struck to announce the entrance of the main actors and at the most important moments in the plot. The loud sound adds to the drama of the performance.

Bonang

A bonang is a percussion instrument from Indonesia. It is played in a traditional gamelan orchestra. It is made up of two rows of small gongs, placed on strings in a wooden frame. The gongs are made from metal and are struck with two padded sticks.

A Gamelan Orchestra

A gamelan is an orchestra mainly made up of percussion instruments. The instruments take great skill to play and must be treated with great respect. For example, people are not allowed to step over the instruments or touch them with their feet. The gamelan plays at religious ceremonies, as well as at dances, traditional puppet shows, and concerts. People make offerings of flowers and incense to the orchestra before it starts playing.

This bonang is being played in Singapore, with a guitar to accompany it.

Musical Notes

A legend from Java tells how the gamelan was invented by King Sang Hyang Guru as a way of talking to the gods.

These musicians in Bali are playing in a gamelan to accompany dancers at a village festival.

Bonang

Small gongs

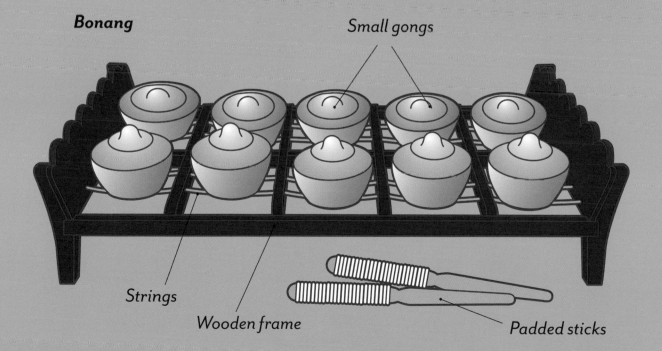

Strings

Wooden frame

Padded sticks

Castanets

Castanets are small, shell-shaped clappers joined together with string. Traditionally, they are made from wood, but fiberglass or plastic is sometimes used today. They are often played by flamenco dancers in Spain to give a lively dancing beat.

String

Wooden clapper

The name "castanets" comes from the Spanish word for chestnut— castaña.

Playing the Castanets

The player uses two pairs of castanets, one in each hand. She hooks the string over her thumb and rests the castanets in her palm, with her fingers bent over. Then she claps her fingers to her palm to make the two pieces of wood clack and click together.

Maracas

Rattles and shakers are percussion instruments that are played all over the world. In South America, rattles, called maracas, are often played to accompany singers and dancers. They are made from hollowed-out gourds or wood, and filled with dried seeds or beads.

Hollow gourd

Dried seeds

Maracas are often played at carnivals and provide a rhythmic beat.

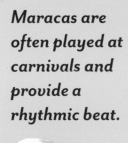

Shaking Maracas

Maracas are some of the easiest instruments to play. A player simply holds a maraca in each hand and gives them a good shake. To get a different sound, the player can also strike the maracas against his arm or leg.

Xylophone

Xylophones have been played all around the world for hundreds of years. These popular percussion instruments are played in traditional music and in orchestras. They make a bright, lively sound and are often the first instruments that children learn to play.

The xylophone player hits the bars with two hard mallets made from plastic, wood, or rubber.

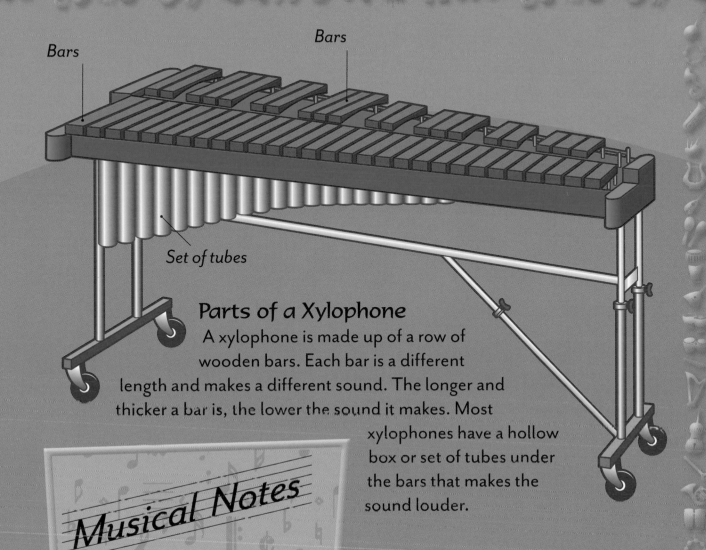

Bars

Bars

Set of tubes

Parts of a Xylophone

A xylophone is made up of a row of wooden bars. Each bar is a different length and makes a different sound. The longer and thicker a bar is, the lower the sound it makes. Most xylophones have a hollow box or set of tubes under the bars that makes the sound louder.

Musical Notes

Some xylophones from Africa have hollowed-out gourds under the bars.

Similar Instruments

Glockenspiels from Germany are similar to xylophones, but they have metal bars instead of wooden ones. Marimbas are instruments from South America. The top set of bars overlaps the bottom set, like the keys of a piano. Marimbas are usually made out of wood, but some are made completely from glass.

Cymbals

Cymbals are percussion instruments that have been played since ancient times. They range from large "crash" cymbals, played in orchestras, to tiny finger cymbals played by dancers. Cymbals are also included in drum sets.

Playing the Cymbals

In a band or orchestra, a cymbal player holds the cymbals apart, then crashes them together. The metal vibrates, producing a loud, dramatic sound. The cymbals can also be brushed together, in an up-and-down movement, to give a softer sound.

The bigger and heavier the cymbals, the louder the sound they make.

Musical Notes

Tiny finger cymbals are used in traditional Middle Eastern music and dancing. The dancer wears one cymbal on her thumb and one on her middle fingers. She strikes them together to make a ringing sound.

Cymbal Shapes

A cymbal is a round piece of metal with a hole drilled in the middle for a strap. The raised part around the hole is called the bell, or dome. It makes a high "pinging" sound when it is hit. The bow is the part around the bell. Crash cymbals come in pairs or as a single cymbal on a stand.

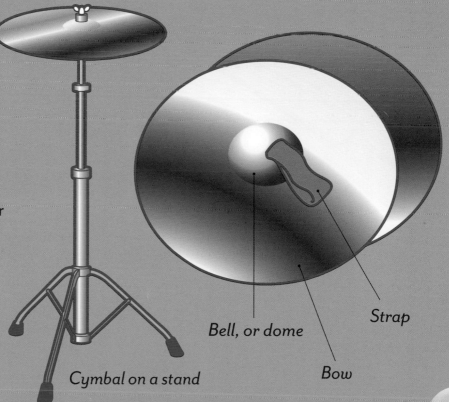

Cymbal on a stand

Bell, or dome

Bow

Strap

Wooden Blocks

Among the simplest percussion instruments of all are wooden blocks that a player hits with sticks, or mallets. They have been played for thousands of years all around the world.

This set of wooden blocks is being played in an orchestra. The blocks are struck with wooden mallets.

Temple Blocks

Temple blocks are large, wooden blocks, carved in the shape of fishes. They are played in China, Japan, and Korea during religious ceremonies in Buddhist temples. They are used to accompany the monks as they chant verses from the sacred texts.

Block Design

The blocks are made from camphor wood. The wood is carved into a round fish shape, then hollowed out inside. Then, the blocks are often painted with red and gold laquer. Some temple blocks can measure more than 1 yard (1 m) across. The bigger the block, the lower the sound it makes. The blocks rest on cushions, so that they do not get damaged.

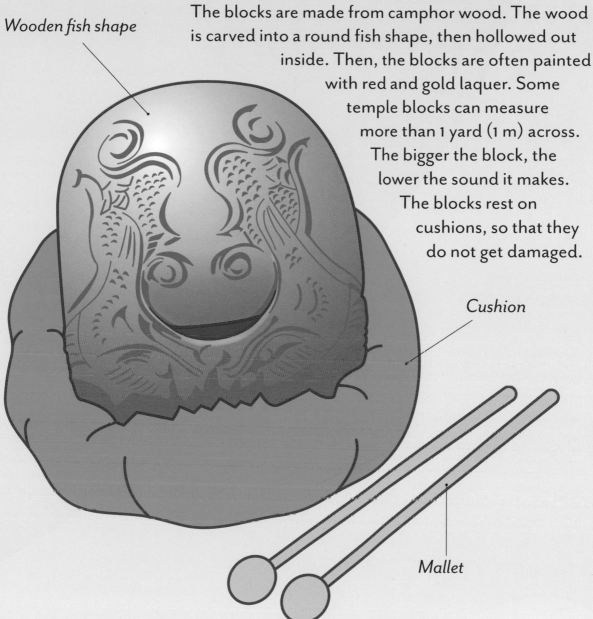

Wooden fish shape

Cushion

Mallet

Musical Notes

Sets of wooden blocks are sometimes played in Western orchestras to copy the sound of horses' hooves.

Words to Remember

brass
a metal that is a mixture of two other metals, copper and zinc; brass instruments are instruments such as trumpets, trombones, and horns

camphor wood
wood from the camphor tree, which grows in Asia

cylinder
a long, tube-like object

festival
an event where people get together to celebrate with singing, dancing, and feasting

fiberglass
a material made from fine fibers of glass

flamenco
a type of dance and music that is popular in some parts of Spain

gourd
a type of fruit with a shell that can be dried and used to make musical instruments

harness
a set of straps worn by a person so that they can carry and play a drum as they are marching

incense
blocks or sticks of spice-like substances that make a sweet smell when they are burned

Indonesia
a country in Southeast Asia

note
a sign that shows the pitch and length of a musical sound

orchestra
a large group of musicians who play a variety of different musical instruments

percussion
a group of musical instruments that make a sound by being hit with sticks or hammers; they include drums, cymbals, and xylophones.

pitch
how high or low a musical note is

rhythm
the regular beat or timing of a piece of music

temple
a building in which followers of some religions worship and hold festivals

vibrate
to move back and forth

woodwind
a group of musical instruments that includes flutes, oboes, and clarinets; a wind instrument makes a sound when it is blown into.

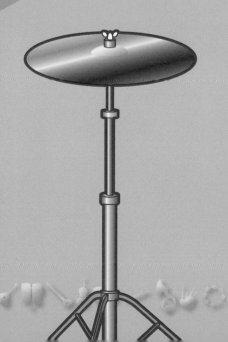

Web Sites

Dallas Symphony Orchestra
http://www.dsokids.com/default.aspx

Play the drums online at Virtual Drumming
http://virtualdrumming.com/

Sphinx Kids! Instrument Storage Room
http://www.sphinxkids.org/Instrument_Storage.html

World Beats by Plunkett Productions
http://www.world-beats.com/

Index

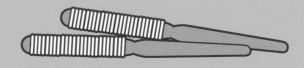